Praise for *Miracle on 31st Street*

A preacher with a motorcycle, cowboy boots, a wicked sense of humor, and a heart that warms you like a huge Southern-style breakfast. That's my pastor!

—Tamron Hall
Broadcast journalist and television host

Susan Sparks has written the best book for our times. She gives us hope, humor and happiness in one neat bundle! It is a joy to read. I highly recommend you read it and share the book with others. Thank you, Susan for your wisdom and humor!

—Catherine A. Allen
Founder and Chairman, The Santa Fe Group
Co-Author, *The Artist Way at Work,*
Reboot Your Life and The Retirement Boom

For most people, Christmas is a noun. It's a December holiday. Sacred for some, commercial for others. For Reverend Susan Sparks, Christmas is also a verb. It's something we <u>do</u> – for self and others – every day of the calendar year. As she demonstrates in *The Miracle on 31st Street*, Christmas means actions that can transform the weary into the wonderful. Through daily exercises, she reminds readers that the hope, peace, love, and joy associated with the yuletide season can re-charge and energize the spirit every day of our lives. Her thought provoking and uniquely persuasive analysis is a must read for all who need this message of hope and healing.

—Katie E. Cherry, PhD
Professor of Psychology, Louisiana State University
Author, *The Other Side of Suffering: Finding a Path to Peace after Tragedy*

Thank you, Reverend Sparks, for reminding us that hope, peace, love, and joy are within us and all around us, even during the most difficult times. *Miracle on 31st Street* is a precious gift, any day of the year.

—Jennifer Haupt, Journalist, *Psychology Today*, "One True Thing" blog

Miracle on 31st Street hits you between the eyes with its practical, real-world epiphanies. Susan Sparks is like a pied piper of hope always reminding us that even in the hardest of times we can still choose joy.

—**Paul Lambert**, Executive Producer of Television,
Film and Stage Musicals, including *The First Wives Club*

Sure life is hard, but it's also a gift. Through her funny, yet inspirational words, Susan Sparks shares how joy and gratitude can be a constant in our lives no matter what the circumstances. Crack open the cover of *Miracle on 31st Street* and reclaim a sense of peace, wonder, awe, and joy—Holiday cheer—every day of the year!

—**Saranne Rothberg**, Health and Happiness Expert, Stage IV Cancer Survivor, Speaker, and Founder, ComedyCures Foundation

Full of uplifting and inspiring stories, *Miracle on 31st Street,* is a total joy. Reverend Susan Sparks once again delights us with her wisdom, warmth and wit. She's masterful. I love reading how to find miracles in my daily life. Thanks, Susan, for leading us down a challenging path and shining a dazzling light.

—**Teri Scheinzeit**, Award-winning Business Coach and Author of *Success Without Stress*

Lord knows, these days we need all the hope, peace, joy, and love we can get—and not just at Christmas. In this powerful book of meditations, Susan Sparks offers profound insights, heart-felt inspiration, and a whole lot of humor so that we can experience the miracles of Christmas whenever we need them, and that means all year long. This book is the best present you could give anyone on your list—especially yourself!

—**The Rev. Peter M. Wallace**, producer and host of "Day1" radio/podcast ministry and author of *The Passionate Jesus* and other books

Miracle On 31st Street

Christmas Cheer Every Day of the Year —
Grinch to Gratitude in 26 Days!

REV. SUSAN SPARKS

FREE GIFTS!

Hi, everyone. I am so excited that you are part of my *Miracle on 31st Street* family!

To welcome you, I have two free gifts:

(1) A printable journal workbook with questions to ponder, and

(2) An online Advent calendar with daily surprises matching each meditation!

Access your calendar and journal from any of these options:

https://mailchi.mp/susansparks.com/freeadventcalendarandjournal

OR

http://susansparks.com/books/miracle-on-31st-street/

OR

or use your smartphone to scan this QR Code:

ALSO BY SUSAN SPARKS:

Laugh Your Way to Grace:
Reclaiming the Spiritual Power of Humor

Preaching Punchlines: The Ten Commandments of Comedy

This book is dedicated to

the children of the Madison Avenue Baptist Church

in New York City,

and to the child in all of us.

ACKNOWLEDGEMENTS

I have so many to thank who were involved in the creation of this book. First, many thanks to the Chautauqua Institution which was willing to go out on a creative limb and host my week-long Christmas in July sermon series in July of 2019. The idea for this book began with those sermons.

I'd also like to thank all those who helped produce and launch *Miracle on 31st Street,* including Lise Cartwright and the other coaches at Self-Publishing School, my editors Amanda Lawrence and Brooks Becker, my marketing copy editor Tania Dakka, my cover designer Christos Angelidakis, my formatter Rachael Cox, and graphic consultant Brace Thompson.

Many thanks to my beautiful community of faith, Madison Avenue Baptist Church in New York City for all their love and support.

And most of all I thank my husband, Toby Solberg, who never fails to lend an "atta girl" when I need it most.

TABLE OF CONTENTS

INTRODUCTION

"Oh, Christmas isn't just a day. It's a frame of mind."

—**Kris Kringle**, *Miracle on 34th Street*

Merry Christmas, y'all!

If you're reading this book during December, my greeting probably sounds normal. However, if you have picked up this book in, say, July, it may sound a bit crazy. Don't let that stop you! This is a book about finding joy and gratitude all year long.

We tend to limit Christmas to the bleak mid-winter—to the twenty-four hours of Santa, packages, trees, and fruitcakes. Then, like good Puritan soldiers, we store our yuletide joy in the attic on December 26th and get back to "real" life. How sad, given that the Christmas spirit is something we desperately need all year long.

For 364 days a year, we are bombarded by stress, commitments, and demands. We face daily worries about our kids, our aging parents, our money, and our future. Every morning we wake up to news of tragedy, violence, and the inhumanity of the world. Yet on one day of the year—Christmas—we are reminded that as a people, we also carry a spark of hope and joy. These are gifts bestowed at birth but often forgotten as life attempts to beat them out of us. Christmas drops a hint of hope in our hearts. Even though it may get covered up or lost in the daily grind, it's ultimately a hint that stays with us, like the balsam tree needles we find six months later behind the couch.

Forgetting the gifts of Christmas can be a dangerous thing. Remember the Grinch who hated Christmas because his heart was two sizes too small? Or Ebenezer Scrooge who lost the ability to feel happiness because he opted for work and money over love and joy? It's easy to make that mistake—to close off our hearts, to opt for "humbug" over happiness—but here's the good news: it's never too late to reclaim the gifts of Christmas. Scrooge found them again. The Grinch found them again. And we can, too.

"Faith is believing in things when common sense tells you not to."

—**Doris Walker**, *Miracle on 34th Street*

The idea for this book originated in a week-long Christmas-in-July sermon series I preached at the historic Chautauqua Institution in upstate New York. Its title was inspired by my community of faith, Madison Avenue Baptist Church, which is located at the corner of 31st Street and Madison Avenue in New York City, just three blocks south of 34th Street and the famous Macy's Department Store of *Miracle on 34th Street* fame.

The book is organized around the four themes of Advent: Hope, Peace, Love, and Joy. Each theme has six daily meditations. There are two additional reflections, one for Christmas Day and one for after Christmas. While the book is built upon a holiday motif, the lessons are universal and have year-round application.

All you have to do is declare that you need some Christmas spirit, designate a block of twenty-six days anytime of the year, and spend a few moments each morning reading the meditations, answering the questions in your journal, and opening your Advent calendar surprise. (You can find instructions on how to access your journal and Advent calendar in the "Free Gifts" section in the beginning of the book.) Experts say you can form a new habit in twenty-one days; I've given you five extra just in case! And what better habit to form than cultivating gratitude and joy?

"I believe, I believe, I believe."

—**Susan Walker,** *Miracle on 34th Street*

This little book is for any time you feel that life has beaten you down and when your belief in miracles is almost gone. It is an antidote for stress, negativity, difficult people, corrosive words, and the feeling that there never is enough time. *Miracle on 31st Street* reminds us that we still have hope, that the world is filled with awe and wonder, that there is great power and healing in silence, that love is most deeply felt when shared, and that we should never postpone our joy.

Okay, maybe hanging Christmas decorations and serving eggnog in July sounds a bit strange, but remembering and celebrating the spirit of Christmas in July, April, October, or December is not crazy at all. In fact, it's absolutely necessary!

Happiness is not a once-a-year event. Christmas is not just a twenty-four-hour holiday. It's a frame of mind. And to honor its gifts and blessings, we must attend to them with gratitude and choose joy all the year long.

HOPE

Am I Gonna Ride This Thing or Not?

"God grant me the serenity to accept the things I cannot change, the courage to change the things I can, and the wisdom to know the difference."

—Reinhold Niebuhr

"God give me the senility to forget the people I didn't like anyway, the good fortune to run into the ones that I do, and the eyesight to tell the difference."

—The Senility Prayer

There are a lot of things that the Bible doesn't tell us.

For instance, what did Jesus do between the ages of twelve and thirty?

Why did God create platypuses before people?

Or this question, with which I have struggled my entire adult life . . .

What did Mary say the split second after Joseph told her that at nine months pregnant, she had to ride a donkey ninety miles up a 2500-foot mountain from Nazareth to Bethlehem in order to answer questions for a census guy? (Luke 2:1-20)

While the Bible doesn't tell us specifically, I don't think God would mind if we read between the lines a little bit. In fact, in imagining what might have been said (and done), we may discover some important lessons of our own.

My best guess at what happened after Joseph's shocking announcement? Mary turned, looked at the donkey, and thought to herself, "Am I gonna ride this thing or not?" In short, do I have a choice in this situation?

We should ask ourselves the same question when faced with difficult circumstances.

Sometimes the answers are crystal clear.

For example, do I need to go to IKEA and wait in line for three hours to buy a bookshelf that will take seventeen hours to put together because it will make my house look slightly more tidy when my relatives visit for thirty minutes?

Answer: No, I'm not riding this.

Do I need to get one more gift for cousin Lu Lu because her stocking looks slightly thinner than cousin Ned's?

Answer: No, I'm not riding this.

Do I need to respond to that personal slight from my work colleague, friend, or family member?

Answer: No, I'm not riding this. (FYI, not everything requires our response.)

These are the easy situations, the ones in which we have full power to say "no."

But sometimes the answers are not so easy. Sometimes we are faced with situations completely out of our control.

Do I have to face down this pandemic?

Answer: Yes, I have to ride this.

Do I have to deal with this grief after my loved one's death?

Answer: Yes, I have to ride this.

Or for Mary, do I have to ride this donkey 90 miles up a 2500-foot mountain?

Answer: Yes, I have to ride this.

Once she realized she had to ride, Mary probably said a second thing to herself: "Better find some padding." Maybe she put a blanket on the donkey, or perhaps she made Joseph shave a sheep to make her a fluffy pillow. Whatever it was, a little padding goes a long way toward easing a bumpy ride—for Mary and for us.

We can find padding in all sorts of places. One source is connecting with people. There's an Ethiopian saying, "When spiders unite, they can tie down a lion." We are all connected through the common web of our humanity. And there is a power in that connection—in feeling part of something. Leverage that power by reaching out to loved ones, friends, and neighbors. Make a phone call, send an email, write a letter. Remember, we are stronger together.

Another place to find padding is perspective. Ask yourself, what is the long view here? What truly matters to me? When I was learning to ride a bike for the first time, my Dad always said, "If you look down, you'll go down." It's also good advice in life. Fixing your gaze up on the goal and not down on the crisis will help you stay balanced and moving forward.

There is a third thing I'm sure happened on that journey (although again, scripture doesn't say it): Mary prayed constantly.

I've often wondered if that trip to Bethlehem marked the invention of the rosary. For every step the donkey took, Mary was probably counting the hairs on his neck, praying each time, "Have mercy."

Sometimes we, too, may feel that way. We hope and pray that every difficult step we take will be the last. We may even think we can't go any further. But when we raise our voices in prayer like Mary did, every angel in heaven comes flying to our aid, and we access a power beyond our pain.

There are things in this life over which we have no control—things that we simply have to get on and ride. But there is a silver lining: if we are riding, we are climbing. And every step we take is a step closer to Bethlehem.

In the end, you never know what can come out of a difficult ride.

Renewed hope? New life? Maybe even a messiah.

It's Still Life

"I expect to pass through this world but once; any good thing therefore that I can do, or any kindness that I can show to any fellow creature, let me do it now; let me not defer or neglect it, for I shall not pass this way again."

—**Stephen Grellet,** *Quaker missionary*

Whining has become an art form in our society. We complain about the winter weather: "Oh my gosh, it's so cold. When will it ever stop?" Six months later, we grumble, "Oh my gosh, it's so hot and humid. When will it ever stop?"

We moan that people are rude during the Christmas rush. We whine that trains and buses are late, that the stock market hasn't done well, or that the grocery store is out of our favorite item. I once heard a woman at Whole Foods complaining to the manager that they were out of her soymilk substitute. First of all, what is soymilk substitute? And second, why would anyone want one, much less have a favorite?

We tend to believe that life comes with a warranty that promises things will always be easy, fun, and painless. When they aren't, we complain incessantly. The truth is that there are no guarantees in life. I recently saw a sign online that said it best. "Life*" was at the top, and the fine print beneath read: "*Available for a limited time only, limit one per customer, subject to change without notice, provided 'as is' without any warranties, your mileage may vary."

We waste so much time complaining about the superficial things that we lose precious seconds, hours, days, even years. As the Jewish prayer says, "Days pass and years vanish, and we walk sightless among miracles." We must be grateful in the good times and the bad, for in the end, it's still life.

The warning "life is short" is often greeted by shrugs and eye rolls. Yes, we've all heard this saying many times, and that's part of the problem. We've heard it so much that we have become immune to the urgency in those three short words.

We don't know what is going to happen from one day to the next. We don't know if we will be given tomorrow or even the rest of today. Look at the headlines: random shootings, suicide bombers, hurricanes and forest fires, soaring cancer statistics.

Life is short.

It is also sacred.

The Psalmists offered this wisdom: "You created my inmost being; you knit me together in my mother's womb . . . I am fearfully and wonderfully made" (Psalm 139:13-14). Life is the greatest, most sacred gift we have. Sure, you may think that the inclement weather or the bus being late or the store being out of your soymilk substitute is important, but if you didn't wake up this morning, then what difference would it make?

Life is short. Life is sacred. And because of that, it should be celebrated in the good times and the bad. No matter where you find yourself—in the long line at the Macy's return counter, in the dentist chair, or in the chemo room—it's still life, and there is joy to be found in the simple act of taking of a breath and acknowledging the gift of the moment.

The author Elisabeth Kübler-Ross wrote, "People are like stained glass windows. They sparkle and shine when the sun is out, but when the darkness sets in, their true beauty is revealed only if there is a light from within."

Find that light. Strive to be grateful in all circumstances. Use your gratitude to inspire and lift up others who are mired in difficulty. We are not guaranteed that life will be easy, fun, or painless. Yet even in the pain, we can be grateful for the profound gift of being alive.

If you find yourself struggling, use these few words as your mantra: "It's still sacred. It's still a gift. It's still life."

The Politics of Sweet Potato Casserole

Those who love to just watch other people work: spec-taters
Those who love to find fault with everyone: commen-taters
Those who love to tell everyone what to do: dic-taters
Those who are always looking to make problems: agi-taters
Those who say they'll help, but never get around to it: hesi-taters
Those who just copy everyone else: imi-taters
Those who give a helping hand without judgment, bringing
love to all they meet: sweet-taters

Way more than politics and religion, my family's passionate holiday fights revolve around food. Specifically, the battle lines are drawn over whether marshmallows or brown sugar and pecans are the best topping for the always wondrous sweet potato casserole.

I, myself, am a brown sugar/pecan warrior, while other, lesser beings in my family believe that white sticky goo should be used as a topping. And so, every year, there's a stand-off. Eyes narrow, arms fold, joy evaporates, and the fight begins.

When you think about it, the actual casserole conflict is pretty lame. Both toppings are sugary, will put you into a diabetic coma with equal speed, and, in the end, will make a great casserole. Surely, somewhere in all this goodness, there has to be a happy medium. There's too much yumminess here to waste on petty infighting.

Sadly, the infighting in our nation is much like my family's sweet potato feud: tragically polarized. It's like the San Andreas fault has jumped out of California and imbedded itself in the hearts of the American people.

We're right; they're wrong. End of story.

Our national perspective is like a greeting card I saw recently that depicted two ladies from the 1950s smoking cigarettes, one saying to the other, "All I know is one of us is right . . . And the other is you."

That is America down to the ground.

What if we come at our conflicts in a different way? What if, instead of a direct marshmallow/brown sugar pecan throwdown, we use the wisdom of St. Francis, who said, "Let me not seek as much . . . to be understood as to understand"?

Conflict resolution experts call this interest-based negotiation, meaning that you focus on why the issue is important to the other side rather than the rightness or wrongness of your respective positions. By identifying shared values, you find common ground, and from that place of commonality, solutions more easily flow.

If I apply this to my family's great marshmallow debate, I quickly see that our shared value is our delight in sweets. We're simply fighting over which ingredients can best lead us to that shared value.

Our political issues can be approached in the same way. In almost every conflict, there is common ground. For example, we all want a better world for our children, fair and equal treatment for our citizens, protection from terrorism, and clean air and water. We're simply fighting over how we get there.

Maybe this holiday, we can consider a new recipe. For our wonderous sweet potato casserole, how about a sugary topping of all three ingredients: marshmallow, brown sugar AND pecans? Or half brown sugar/pecan and half marshmallow? Or how about we use neither and top the sweet potatoes with Cap'n Crunch?

We can also consider a new recipe for this nation and this world—a wondrous casserole of ethnicities, races, and religions. We need a fresh approach that focuses on our commonalities and then finds a way to combine our needs, hopes, and dreams into a dish that feeds us all. Let's celebrate and give thanks for what we share as a family and a global community. Surely, somewhere in all this goodness, there has to be a happy medium.

It Takes Heat to Bring the Grace

"Nothing ever goes away until it teaches us
what we need to know."

—Pema Chodron

I've had the privilege of visiting two holy shrines in my life: The Church of the Nativity in Bethlehem and Eugene's Hot Chicken in Birmingham, Alabama. The first shrine is self-explanatory. Hopefully, the second is as well, but for those of you who don't know about hot chicken, my condolences. It's one of God's greatest inventions. You fry up chicken nice and crispy, and then right as it comes out of the fryer, you pour on some hot sauce that seeps into the batter.

Everybody prepares it differently. Eugene's, for example, has four different levels of hot: southern (no heat), mild, hot, and what they call "stupid hot."

When I reached this holy chicken shrine, I stood in line, pondering which heat level to order. Just as I was about to say, "Hot," I heard a voice behind me say, "get the stupid hot."

I turned around, and standing there was a local elderly woman (I knew she was local because she pronounced the word "hot" with two syllables).

"Really?" I asked. "Should I go that hot?"

With a mischievous look in her eye, she smiled and replied, "Well, as I've always said, it takes heat to bring the grace."

Honey, she was exactly right. After the fire of my first bite subsided, grace descended like a dove. Grace . . . and heartburn, but grace nonetheless.

I learned an important lesson at Eugene's that afternoon: good things can come from moments of fire. The Bible shares the same lesson in the story of Jacob wrestling with an angel-type figure in Genesis. Rather than give up, Jacob holds on and does something audacious. He looks the figure in the eye and says, "I won't let go until you give me a blessing!"

The nerve! Yet, what happens? God gives him that blessing: a new name—Israel— which translates to "God prevails." By refusing to let the struggle defeat him, Jacob turns it into a blessing, something that makes him stronger for the days ahead.

What do you wrestle with in your life? What "stupid hot" things are you facing right now? What would happen if you took hold of one of those issues, looked it in the eye, and said, "I won't let go until you give me a blessing?"

Do you face a job loss? Perhaps you would receive a blessing of faith. Are you facing a medical crisis? Maybe you would receive a blessing of courage. Do you have a relationship problem? Perhaps you would receive a blessing of humility. Even with something as minor as waiting to return a holiday gift at Best Buy, asking for a blessing might bring you a lesson in patience.

In the end, we're all trying to be better people, striving to be more like our creator. And perhaps God is offering us a little help through situations that challenge us.

There's an old myth in metalworking that says a silversmith knows the metal is fully refined when he can see his reflection in it. Perhaps God is doing the same: refining us through fire not only to make us stronger, but also to make us better reflect our creator's image.

Consider the possibility that each hardship in life comes bearing a divine blessing. Rather than turn from it, wrestle with it. Look it in the eye, and face the fire.

Demand a blessing.

Hey, who knows what might happen? Like with Eugene's hot chicken, sometimes it takes heat to bring the grace.

A Place Called Grace

"Laughter is the closest thing to the grace of God."

—Karl Barth

I need to say a little more about grace.

Some days, I have an inordinate need for "grace." And by "grace," I mean the theological concept, but even more so, I mean my grandmother. A tiny, rather squishy woman, "Ganny" gave hugs that felt like being pressed into a fluffy feather pillow.

I called her "Ganny" because I had trouble pronouncing all three syllables of "grand-mo-ther." That was ironic, given that my other grandmother, a woman of German and Scots-Irish descent, required all three syllables to be pronounced along with her last name: "Grand-mo-ther Whit-mire." (While I adored them both, their naming preference should tell you something about the difference in the two women.)

Ganny lived with "Grand-dad" (I could manage those two syllables) in a modest little house next to the A&P Grocery in Gaffney, South Carolina, and thanks to that grocery, I'll always remember the weekly visits we made to their home, especially at the holidays.

Upon our arrival, Ganny would grab me up in an inordinately long, squishy hug and call me "her precious little thing." (Given my behavior at that age, the accuracy of that statement was highly doubtful.) Then she would scurry me off to the kitchen to enjoy some kind of treat, like cherry pie filling from the A&P. Ganny knew that I didn't like pie crust, so she would peel away the shell and feed me spoonfuls of the cherry insides. (Yes, I know. Don't even say it.)

While her nickname was "Ganny," my grandmother's real name was Grace—Grace Foster Sparks. In fact, I was named after her (Susan Grace Sparks). And while the great theologians like Martin Luther and St. Augustine have attempted to describe grace in deep theological ways, I believe the home of Grace Foster Sparks provides the best image of all.

To me, grace is not necessarily a thing, but a place—a place of grounding and belonging where you feel special, like you're wrapped in an inordinately long, squishy hug, eating the filling out of a pie.

We all need to find that place. Every day we are bombarded by corrosive voices from the world outside and from inside our own hearts. We are assaulted by words that slowly tear us down, shrink us in shame, and make us feel less than the beloved children of God that we are. We need to find that place called grace.

One of the best places to find it is in scripture. In fact, I've put together a list of what I like to call "squishy scriptures"—Bible verses that make me feel like I am wrapped in an inordinately long, squishy hug, eating the filling out of a pie. I have included my list below.

I hope that you will take a moment throughout your week to pause and read them, reminding yourself that you are called as God's precious one. Then spread that joy. Think about three people who need to hear from you. Perhaps a family member, friend, spouse, or even stranger needs your words. Share a hug or a some "pie-filling" kindness with someone to remind them of their divinity as a child of God.

While I miss sitting in Ganny's kitchen eating A&P pie, her legacy lives on, and through that memory, I learned that living a life of love and beauty is not that hard, even in these difficult times. It's all about recalling who we are. It's all about remembering from whence we came.

It's all about finding a place called grace.

Squishy Scriptures

Isaiah 41:10 "Do not fear, for I am with you; do not anxiously look about you, for I am your God. I will strengthen you, surely, I will help you, surely, I will uphold you with My righteous right hand."

2 Timothy 1:7 "For God did not give us a spirit of timidity, but of power and of love and of calm and well-balanced mind and discipline and self-control."

Psalm 55:22 "Cast your burden on the Lord and He will sustain you; He will never allow the righteous to be moved."

Exodus 23:20 "I am going to send an angel in front of you, to guard you on the way."

Psalm 62:6 "He only is my Rock and my Salvation; He is my Defense and my Fortress, I shall not be moved."

Isaiah 43:1-2 "Do not fear, for I have redeemed you; I have called you by name, you are mine. When you pass through the waters, I will be with you; and through the rivers, they shall not overwhelm you; when you walk through fire you shall not be burned, and the flame shall not consume you."

Psalm 57:1 "Be merciful to me, O God, be merciful to me, for in you my soul takes refuge; in the shadow of your wings I will take refuge, until the destroying storms pass by."

2 Kings 20:5 "Thus says the LORD, the God of David your father: I have heard your prayer, I have seen your tears; surely, I will heal you."

Isaiah 40:31 "But they that wait upon the Lord shall renew their strength; they shall mount up with wings as eagles; they shall run, and not be weary, and they shall walk and not faint."

Philippians 4:6-7 "Do not be anxious about anything, but in everything, by prayer and petition, with thanksgiving, present your requests to God. And the peace of God, which transcends all understanding, will guard your hearts and your minds in Christ Jesus."

Isaiah 41:10 "So do not fear, for I am with you; do not be dismayed, for I am your God. I will strengthen you and help you; I will uphold you with my righteous right hand."

Psalm 91:11 "For he will command his angels concerning you to guard you in all your ways. On their hands they will bear you up, so that you will not dash your foot against a stone."

A Star is Born

"When we contemplate the whole globe as one great
dewdrop, striped and dotted with continents and islands,
flying through space with other stars all singing and shining
together as one, the whole universe appears as an infinite
storm of beauty."

—John Muir

Given the title of this piece, I'd like to qualify something upfront: I am not trying to do a mash-up of the movie *A Star is Born* and Christmas. That would be too creepy, especially with the 1976 version. Barbara Streisand as Mary? Kris Kristofferson as Joseph? And the baby Jesus played by a young Gary Busey? That's just wrong.

No, I'm talking about real stars, the kind that shine from the sky, not the stage.

For thousands of years, humanity has been drawn to the light of the stars. We watch the constellations, track the paths of the planets, and study the cycle of the sun, all in an attempt to understand the great mysteries of life. NASA does it, Galileo did it, and 2000 years ago, the three Wise Men did it. They tracked the stars to find the Messiah.

But the draw of the heavens for us is more than simple imagination or exploration. It is organic, even hereditary. The stars are our old ones, our wise ones, for we as human beings carry their genetic imprint. Joni Mitchell sang the famous lyrics "we are stardust," and as it turns out, she's right.

Literally.

Our human bodies are made of remnants of stars and massive explosions in the galaxies. Carbon, nitrogen, oxygen, iron, and sulfur—most of the materials that we're made of—come out of the star dust kicked off by those explosions and scattered across the universe. As Astrophysicist Karel Schrijver explained in *National Geographic*, "We have stuff in us as old as the universe."

In fact, there is a striking parallel between the life cycle of a star and the spiritual life cycle of human beings. (Brace yourself—a liberal arts major is about to explain physics . . .)

There are basically two stages to the life of a star. The first stage is when a star is born. As gravity begins to pull gases towards a center core, the temperature begins to rise, and eventually, the density of the gases causes a nuclear reaction. It's then that the star begins to shine, drawing energy toward the light, to its core, then radiating that light back out into the galaxy.

This can go on for billions of years until we come to the second stage, when the star's center can no longer hold. Because the star has too little fuel left to maintain its core temperature, its light goes out and it collapses under its own weight, drawing everything around it into a dark abyss.

Tell me that doesn't sound familiar. Sometimes we draw our energy toward the light and reflect its warmth to all around us. Other times, we have lost all fuel; our light goes out and we collapse, emotionally or otherwise, into a dark abyss.

These days, it's easy to find ourselves in that abyss. Between crazy schedules, job stress, money worries, health issues, concerns for our children, and worries for our world, it's easy to find ourselves drawn to the darkness. And like the stars, the only thing between a heart that draws in the light and a heart that collapses into a black hole is a strong center that can hold.

Sadly, we tend to put all kinds of crazy things at our center that weaken our core, such as ego, anger, resentment, and fear. We lean on titles, bank accounts, status, and stuff. We look to other people—to our spouses, partners, friends, and family—to fill our core.

Inevitably, there comes a time when these things can't hold anymore. The job won't last forever. The money gets spent. Botox lasts for only three months (or so I've heard). Like a dying star, we begin to collapse into the darkness when our center can't hold, and the light goes out.

We must find a center that will hold, and that center is God. We need look no further than the scriptures for confirmation. Take, for example, Isaiah 40:31: "But they that wait upon the Lord shall renew their strength; they shall mount up with wings as eagles."

What do you have at the center of your life?

Is it strong enough to hold you through the good times and the bad?

If your center is not holding, if your light is starting to go out, walk outside this evening. Find a place where you can look up into the heavens and see the stars. Remember how they transform chaos and turmoil into light. Remember how their warmth and power radiate far out into the universe. And most importantly, remember that it was a star that pulled the Wise Men towards the true light of world.

We have the power to shine as brightly as those stars. All we have to do is find a center that will hold. All we have to do is find the place in our hearts where a star is born.

PEACE

Lessons from a Christmas Cactus

"The darkest nights produce the brightest stars."

—John Green

Don't you think it's odd that the time of year when we celebrate the light of the world—the Christ child—is also the darkest time of year? At least here in the Northern Hemisphere, you get up in the morning, and it's dark. You leave work, and it's dark. Somewhere in the middle, it gets light, but you don't remember 'cause you're too busy complaining about how dark it is all the time.

As mere human beings, we find it hard to wait for the light of the world during the darkest time of the year. However, if we were, say, a Christmas cactus, it would be easy.

Every December, Emma Sue Whitmire (my grandmother who preferred all the syllables of her name to be pronounced) used to display huge hanging baskets of Christmas cactuses that were inordinately loaded with red blooms. We couldn't figure out how she did it, until one day, she shared her trick. She put them in the cold, dark root cellar during the rest of the year. In short, the plants learned to thrive in the darkness.

Maybe we should take a lesson from the Christmas cactus during this Advent season. Life can be found in the darkest of times and places. In fact, that is where life bursts forth.

This may sound counterintuitive because we tend to think of darkness as negative, bad, or evil. However, that belief provides an important lesson on the power of words. We should be careful about the language we use because what we say over time affects what we do and how we think. For example, if we consistently speak of darkness as evil or bad, how can we help translating that into our views on race? We must question our own thinking by closely observing the world around us.

There are infinite examples of the goodness and beauty of darkness. For example, the black ink on this page ushers in a new world of words. Black clothing can slim even the worst of holiday excesses. Then there's the sheen of a raven's wing in the noonday sun; the deep, dark haze of the Blue Ridge mountains; or the most obvious example of beauty in darkness . . . chocolate.

Darkness is also a source of life itself. It was God's first creation: "In the beginning when God created the heavens and the earth, the earth was a formless void, and darkness covered the face of the deep" (Genesis 1:1-2). Night is when all life sleeps and rejuvenates. Human life begins in the darkness of the womb, and seeds germinate in the deep darkness of the earth.

The dark can even bring sight—literal and figurative. Consider the human eye, which has a light part and a dark part. Our vision comes from the dark part. Darkness also brings figurative sight—insight—as human beings need dormancy, rest, and darkness to create, thrive, and flower.

What beautiful new thing do you want to birth in the darkness of this Advent season?

Where in your life do you want to blossom?

Next time you get up in the dark and go to bed in the dark and wonder when, if ever, the light will come, remember the beauty and life that can be found in darkness. Use this time of quiet and dormancy to ponder the wonders of the season. Think about what you want to grow. Because soon, almost imperceptibly, light will begin to gleam forth from a star in the heavens, and the world will rejoice in the birth of a king.

It Wasn't Exactly a Silent Night

"And the Grinch, with his Grinch-feet ice cold in the snow, stood puzzling and puzzling, how could it be so? It came without ribbons. It came without tags. It came without packages, boxes, or bags. And he puzzled and puzzled 'till his puzzler was sore. Then the Grinch thought of something he hadn't before. What if Christmas, he thought, doesn't come from a store? What if Christmas, perhaps, means a little bit more?"

—**Dr. Seuss,** *How the Grinch Stole Christmas!*

On Christmas Eve, people all over the world will gather together, light candles, and sing "Silent Night," marking this as a time of beauty, peace, and silence. But I wonder—if we found ourselves back in that manger in Bethlehem 2000 years ago, would it fit our expectations? I mean, given the reality of that situation, it wasn't exactly a silent night.

We all know the story. Caesar called for a census, forcing everyone to go back to their own city to register. As a result, Joseph had to haul himself and his pregnant wife from Galilee to Bethlehem. (This was, of course, after Mary decided she was gonna ride that donkey in the first place.)

Given that the journey to Bethlehem is straight up a mountainside, we can assume that everyone was in a bad mood that night: Joseph having to pull the donkey up the slope, Mary having to ride that donkey while pregnant, and the donkey having to haul everyone and their stuff up a mountain.

If that wasn't enough, they had to spend the night (all of them in their respective bad moods) in a barn. Not an inn, not a Days Inn, not even a Budget Inn. A barn, where all the animals of the inn were kept.

Imagine the scene as they all settled in for this "silent" night: there was the donkey that had climbed a couple of thousand feet with a pregnant woman (*heehaw, heehaw*), Joseph snoring up a storm because he was exhausted *(ZZZzzzz)*, the sheep mad at Joseph's snoring (*baaaa*), camels mad at the sheep (camel noise— whatever that is), chickens mad in general (*bwok, bwok, BWOK)*, and, of course, in a few minutes, you add a woman having a baby.

Now, I know this was Holy Mother Mary, but without an epidural, even Mary might have had a few sounds to add. So, you get *heehaw, ZZZzzzz, baaaa,* camel noise, *bwok bwok BWOK,* JOSEPHHHHH!!!

It wasn't exactly a silent night.

Of course, this is not an alien concept to us in the twenty-first century because we, too, are living in the chaos of a barnyard, and the noise is deafening.

For many of us, that chaos is in our personal lives. It's in our mammoth to-do lists, our family and relationship conflicts, the heartbreak or loss or loneliness that many of us feel. It's in the fleeting, unpredictable nature of our health or that of a loved one. Every day, these stressors, pains, and demands shout at us from all sides.

One of the loudest barnyard noises in our lives comes from our electronics. The electronic revolution has utterly destroyed our ability to tap into our own peace. New York University Professor Dr. Adam Alter calls smartphones "adult pacifiers" and explains that the average adult spends between eleven and fifteen years of life looking at a screen.

The Prince of Peace—our personal peace—our gift, our connection to the holy, is not "out there" in an app, podcast, or smartphone. It's not in the barnyard chaos of our world. It's in the silence within.

But there is good news in the midst of this noisy chaos. After the cacophony of the donkey, the sheep, Joseph, the camel, the chickens, and Mary giving birth, there was one last sound . . . that of a tiny baby.

In that moment, that chaotic barn got silent really fast. All eyes turned toward Mary and the manger. Nothing was heard. Nothing was said, and nothing needed to be said, for all who were there knew that the world had just changed. In the chaos of that barnyard, a prince of peace had been born.

Although we may live in the chaos of a barnyard, the noise of that barnyard is not the end of the story. Today, we are invited into that quiet place again, into that transition from barnyard to beauty, from chaos to silence. It is a gift for us not only at Christmas, but every day of our lives. We simply have to slow down, quiet ourselves, and listen for that faint cry of the newborn Christ, for in it we find the beauty and healing of a true silent night.

"And, lo, the angel of the Lord came upon them,
and the glory of the Lord shone round about them:
and they were sore afraid.
And the angel said unto them,
Fear not: for, behold, I bring you good tidings of great joy,
which shall be to all people.
For unto you is born this day in the city of David
a Savior, which is Christ the Lord" (Luke 2:9-11).

Lord, I'll Bail the Boat. You Calm the Storm.

"I've learned that you can tell a lot about a person by the way (s)he handles these three things: a rainy day, lost luggage, and tangled Christmas tree lights."

—Maya Angelou

I'm convinced that the primary goal of every strand of holiday lights is to instigate human fury. I know this from personal experience. At the end of each Christmas season, I spend hours winding the lights into neat, orderly coils. Then, in an effort to spite me, those vindictive wee lights manage to unwrap themselves sometime during the next eleven months and engage in a hurricane-like spinning dance, knotting their wires into a mass of mayhem.

Every year on that fateful day in early December when I reach into the closet to bring down the sack of Christmas lights, I can hear them tittering and giggling in anticipation of my reaction. It's then that I put down the bag and head to the Gospel of Luke to find solace in Jesus' calming of the storm.

After a long day of teaching, Jesus and his disciples are in a small boat on the Sea of Galilee. A furious storm blows in, and as the boat begins to swamp, the disciples begin to panic. (Please keep in mind that at least four of them were professional fishermen, so this must have been one honkin' storm.)

The scripture doesn't tell us this specifically, but I imagine that when the boat starts to fill with water, the disciples do the one thing they can do—bail out the boat. They bail and bail, yet the water keeps coming, and the wind keeps howling. Finally, when the boat is about to sink, they call for Jesus, who is asleep in the stern (quite a feat in such a tumult): "Teacher, do you not care that we are perishing?"

Jesus stands up, rebukes the wind, then says to the sea, "Peace! Be still!" The wind ceases, and there is a dead calm on the waters. Then Jesus says, "Why are you so afraid? Do you still have no faith?" (Mark 4:40).

What strikes me about this story is the distinct nature of the roles of the disciples and Jesus. The disciples are in charge of sailing the boat and bailing it out when it starts to sink. That's what they can do. That is in their control. On the other hand, Jesus is in charge of calming the storm. That is within his control.

It's the same for us. We, as human beings, are best suited for sailing and bailing the boat—for showing up, putting in the time, and doing the work. That is in our control. Jesus, on the other hand, is best for calming the storms—for easing our fears, doubts, anger, and resentment. That is within his control.

The problem is that we usually try to do Jesus' job as well as our own, which doesn't work. The great jazz singer Lena Horne explained it like this: "It's not the load that breaks you down. It's how you carry it."

That's why I've now started keeping two to-do lists: one for myself and one for Jesus.

Here's an example. Let's say you have a medical issue. Your to-do list should be about sailing and bailing the boat—which means doing things within your control, such as going to the doctor, taking your meds, and undergoing the necessary tests or treatments. Jesus' to-do list should contain things that you don't do so well or that aren't in your control, things like worrying about what tomorrow will bring.

Are you anxious about money? Your to-do list is to sail and bail the boat: make a budget, cut down on costs, and pay down or renegotiate your debt. Things to put on Jesus' list: calm the storm of apprehension and ease the stigma of shame.

Or maybe you are trying to untangle an unruly gang of Christmas lights. Your list: sit down and unwind the cords. Jesus' list: still the urge to fling them out the window.

We all face storms in this life, some on the level of tangled holiday lights, and others existential. Whatever the storms, we must remember that they can be calmed at any time. It all comes down to splitting your to-do list into the two categories reflected in this simple prayer:

"Lord, I'll bail the boat. You calm the storm."

Shabbat? Why Not!

"Almost everything will work again if you unplug it for a few minutes . . . including you."

—Anonymous

One of the last things we think about during the holidays is self-care. Really, how could we possibly prioritize it? There are mountains of yummy high-cholesterol things to eat and our to-do lists are seventy pages long. At some point, however, we have to pause and refuel, or we'll never get through this marathon we call Christmas (or life).

One of the best lessons in self-care I ever experienced was from a tiny silver-haired woman with a twinkle in her eye. Her name was Nana Gert, and she was the grandmother of a dear friend. I met her many years ago when I first moved from North Carolina to New York. Upon hearing that I was new in town and that I had no family in the area, Nana Gert insisted on inviting me, a Baptist from the South, to her famous Friday Shabbat dinners on Long Island.

Each week, I would gather with her family around her table, which simply groaned under the weight of matzo ball soup, veal cutlets, and noodle kugel. Marveling at how Nana Gert, who was in her mid-eighties, had the energy to prepare such a huge dinner every week, I finally asked her for her secret. She explained it like this:

"Traditionally, Jews celebrate Shabbat on Friday evenings into Saturday, but at my age, I need a break—a Shabbat—more than once a week! So, whenever I'm tired, whether it be on a Friday or a Monday or a Wednesday, I sit down and declare, 'Shabbat? Why not!'"

All these years later, her words still strike me as so very true. For Christians and Jews alike, keeping the Sabbath holy is a commandment and a blessing from God: "Then God blessed the seventh day and made it holy, because on it he rested from all the work of creating that he had done" (Genesis 2:3).

Her words also make practical sense today. In our fast-paced world, one weekly Shabbat may not be enough. Why limit ourselves? We have the power to claim Shabbat anytime, anywhere we need it! While it may be nice to take a six-month cruise through the Greek Isles, a one-minute Shabbat pause during a busy workday can sometimes be just as rejuvenating. Simply give yourself permission to take a break, whether it be physical, emotional, or spiritual.

A physical break is easy. Just go on a short walk, stretch, or take a few deep breaths. Studies show that a simple five-minute break from your desk can substantially increase your energy and efficiency and reduce your stress levels.

An emotional break is equally easy. Sometimes it is simply a matter of managing your expectations. Take a Shabbat from demanding perfection from yourself and those around you.

Billy Graham's wife, Ruth Graham, knew the power of this lesson. On a ride back from one of her husband's crusades, Ruth saw a sign indicating road work. She requested the words of that sign be her epitaph. Today, her memorial reads, "End of construction.

Thank you for your patience." We are all just human, doing the best we can.

Shabbat can also mean taking a moment to meditate or pray. This could be anywhere; you don't have to be in a church or synagogue or Nepalese monastery. Taking a spiritual Shabbat break is like charging your cell phone; you are simply taking a moment to access that which empowers you.

Sadly, many of us believe that not working non-stop makes us lesser people. Perhaps we were made to feel that we don't deserve to rest or to take care of ourselves. Somewhere along the way, we began to believe that if we were less productive, we would be less loved, as if love were based on a market economy.

In the end, what are the times in our lives that we will remember? Not the board meetings or the political rallies or the committee meetings or the checks on our to-do list. We will remember times we spent around a table with friends or family; times we engaged in activities about which we are passionate; and times we renewed ourselves, gaining perspective and healing.

To this day, I still can't cook a lovely dinner like Nana Gert could, but I'm getting better at cooking up the gift of time for myself. This holiday season, why not consider giving and receiving the same gift in your life? Give yourself permission to take a break. Honor God's commandment to rest. Remember the wisdom of Nana Gert: No matter what the day of the week, if you're tired, stop, pause, and declare to all the world, "Shabbat? Why not!"

Lord, Give Me Patience . . . and Make It Snappy!

"Patience is not simply the ability to wait—it's how we behave while we're waiting."

—Joyce Meyer

Our modern society can best be described in three words: fast, immediate, and instant! We speed walk, speed dial, and speed date. We disdain anything that takes extra time, including the US mail, which we affectionately call "snail mail" (an ironic nickname, given that 150 years ago, mail delivered by horseback was called "the pony express").

We even speed pray. Recently, while waiting in an inordinately long line at Target for Christmas wrapping paper, I mumbled through gritted teeth, "Lord, give me patience." Almost without thinking, I then added, "and make it snappy!"

It's hard to have patience in a sound bite world. That said, it is a virtue worth cultivating. We see this lesson over and over in scripture.

Consider Hebrews 12:1: "Let us run with patience the race that is set before us." In short, life's a marathon, so pace yourself.

Patience may be one of the best things we can do for our stamina and our health. Exhibit A: my Dad, Herb. A twentieth-century Buddha with a North Carolina accent, Herb was never in a hurry. Nothing ruffled him, and nothing fazed him. His heart rate stayed the same (roughly seven beats per minute) through thick and thin. Even though he lived on a diet of fried chicken, cream gravy, Frito scoops, and pecan pie, Herb made it to the ripe old age of eighty-nine. Why? Because he was *patient*. It's like the old saying goes, "It's better to be patient, than to become one."

Patience also brings perspective. "Let every person be quick to hear, slow to speak, slow to anger" (James 1:19). Similar advice came from a partner in my old law firm. He used to say, "Always wait twenty-four hours before firing off an angry response." That suggestion has saved me from much unnecessary angst.

How many times have you fired off an email or a text in a knee-jerk reaction that you regretted, or spewed out words that you wish you could take back? With the buffer of time, you might have been able to see the issue or the person differently. In the end, what's the downside of waiting to respond? If it's that big of an issue, it'll be there tomorrow.

The opportunity for growth is perhaps the most important gift we receive from practicing patience. The Bible says, "Be patient, then, brothers and sisters . . . See how the farmer waits for the land to yield its valuable crop, patiently waiting for the autumn and spring rains" (James 5:7). It's too bad that we don't treat others like farmers treat their crops, enabling their growth through patient tending.

Too often we get impatient with people—finishing their sentences, tuning out if they take too long to tell a story, or taking over their jobs if they don't do the work quickly enough or in the way that we want.

The author Paulo Coelho tells the story of a man watching a butterfly struggling to emerge from its cocoon. The man decides to help the butterfly by cutting open the cocoon to free it. What he fails to realize is that the effort required to break free from the cocoon is nature's way of strengthening the butterfly's wings. In trying to accelerate the process, the man destroys the butterfly's ability to fly.

Similarly, we can clip people's wings through our own impatience. It takes time for people to strengthen and grow into their potential. We must have the patience to allow them that time.

When you feel your patience waning, ask yourself: Is this worth my health? In twenty-four hours, will my perspective change? Is this something or someone that needs extra time to develop fully?

Patience is a virtue worth cultivating. Try it. Just breathe. Take a beat before you respond. Be gentle with those you love. And if all else fails, use this simple prayer to get yourself started: "Lord give me patience . . . and make it snappy!"

Wasting Time with God

"Listen to silence. It has so much to say."

—Rumi

Sometimes for Christmas, I'll return to my childhood home in Charlotte, North Carolina. It's funny how when you return home, the memories start pouring in. For example, as the plane was landing on one of my last visits, I spied an old, abandoned parking lot with weeds and broken asphalt at the end of the runway. Seconds later, as the plane touched down, images of my childhood began to emerge.

My dad and I would hang out in that old parking lot on lazy Saturday afternoons, sitting in our lawn chairs, eating peanuts, and watching the planes come and go. While to some that may sound pedestrian, we loved it. It was our time, quality time with just us— no agenda, nothing to do, nowhere to go. We didn't even say that much. It was simply wasting time watching the planes—together.

In thinking back on that memory, I began to realize that "wasting time" with those you love is, perhaps, one of the most important things you can do. Spending unstructured time together helps you reconnect, bond, and build intimacy, honesty, and trust. It makes you stronger.

So, if it's so important in our human relationships, why don't we ever talk about wasting time with God? I'm talking about quality time with God—no agenda, nothing to do, nowhere to go, not even saying that much. Just wasting time together.

Thanks to our modern-day views of efficiency, wasting time with God may strike many as a bad thing. Our society is all about multitasking, results, and getting a lot done in a short amount of time. Our mantra is "To do more is to have more, and to have more is to be more."

The Internet has exacerbated the issue. Recently, I discovered some mind-bending statistics: 281 billion emails are sent each day, and over 200,000 text messages are sent per second. Think about the amount of information that comes through your computer and phone every day. To survive in this crazy cyber world, we have to be able to multitask with lightning efficiency.

And so, in this giant cyber gerbil wheel of efficiency, we relegate God to the times and places that we see as productive and useful, such as church. Church is very efficient—you meet God for an hour, see your friends, have a cup of coffee, and you're done for the week.

Don't get me wrong. I love the church, and as an ordained minister, I have dedicated my life to the church. But if you consign God to only one hour a week, from 11 a.m. –12 p.m. on Sunday, that leaves 167 other hours. One out of 168 is not the ratio of someone who prioritizes the holy.

In her book *An Altar in the World: A Geography of Faith*, theologian and priest Barbara Brown Taylor argues that the whole world is the house of God: "Earth is so thick with divine possibility that it is a wonder we can walk anywhere without cracking our shins on altars."

She then tenders these two poignant questions: "Do we build God a house so that we can choose when to go see God? Do we build God a house in lieu of having God stay at ours?"

The world is so full of opportunities to draw near to and "waste time" with God. Yet we continue to prioritize productivity. News flash: the value of our lives has nothing to do with whether we're efficient or productive. Our innate worth was given to us the second we were born, and no one can take that away.

Waste a little time with those you love, including God. Intentionally leave unscheduled gaps in your day—time that has little to do with attaining or achieving but everything to do with building and bonding. Commit to time with no agenda, nothing to do, and nowhere to go, when you don't even say that much.

Remember, God is with us every moment, waiting and longing to spend time with us. As James 4:5 teaches, "God yearns jealously for the spirit that he has made to dwell in us." Make that relationship your priority. Give God the gift of more than 1:168. Pledge to yourself: I will make time—to waste time—with God.

LOVE

Pray Like a Telemarketer

Tell me if this sounds familiar: You come home at the end of a long day, hoping for a little peace and quiet. You change into some comfy clothes, click on Netflix to watch *Rudolph* or *Scrooge*, then—of course—the phone rings, and an enthusiastic voice on the other end chirps, "Hi! You've just won a timeshare in south Florida!"

Ah, telemarketers—one of God's great mysteries and the number-one complaint of consumers. Whether they are salespeople pushing timeshares in Florida or politicians trying to get votes, these interminable, unceasing, relentless robocalls never stop.

Will we ever get our peace and quiet? Who knows, but as the old saying goes, "If you can't beat 'em, join 'em." So I say, let's learn something from their tactics.

The Bible gives us an example of how to do this in the book of Luke. There Jesus offers a parable to show how we should pray and never give up. The story involves an unjust judge who neither fears God nor has respect for people and a widow who constantly—relentlessly—pesters the judge for justice (a telemarketer kind of approach). The widow eventually wears him down, and the judge gives in (Luke 18:1-8).

So, Jesus is saying that we should pray like a telemarketer? Really?

I guess one could argue that with all the billions of prayers going up, we need to pray relentlessly in order to be heard, especially this time of year with prayers of Christmas, Hanukah, and Kwanza crowding the airwaves.

But honestly, I can't see Jesus saying that we need to pray like a telemarketer to be heard. I think the parable is about something deeper—about how consistent, unceasing prayer can soften even the hardest heart.

Think about it like this: If we are sick and a doctor prescribes a course of antibiotics, we don't take one pill, then ask, "Why am I not cured?" We take the whole course. And we take it consistently. Why? Because we trust the doctor who prescribed it.

Prayer operates the same way. God prescribes it. For example, in Jeremiah 29:12, God says, "Then you will call on me and come and pray to me, and I will listen to you." We can't raise up one prayer, then say, "Why am I not healed?" Prayer is a course of medicine because we are the ones who are sick—we are the ones who need our hearts softened, our eyes opened, and our minds changed about how we see and treat others.

Some of you may argue, "My heart is not hardened. I pray and serve God." Good for you, but that's only half the formula. It's no accident that the unjust judge in our story is described as someone who cares for neither God nor others. Those two things are inextricably bound. Remember the words in 1 John 4:20: "If someone says, 'I love God,' and hates his brother, he is a liar; for the one who does not love his brother whom he has seen, cannot love God whom he has not seen."

Some of you may also be thinking, "I want to pray for others, but I'm in pain. I need help, too." Praying for someone else is a way to heal both of you at the same time. The act of focusing outside yourself simultaneously blesses those you pray for and brings you a perspective and purpose that take your mind off your own situation.

And of course there's always the people that say, "I just don't have time to pray." My friend, and author, Peter Shankman offers this challenge: replace all instances of "I don't have the time to" with "I don't have the desire to." That puts things in laser perspective. For example, you might say you don't have time to pray in the morning. Translated that means you don't have the desire to pray in the morning. Interesting, since you do have the time (the desire) in the morning to turn on your phone, read news, emails, texts, Facebook posts, make coffee, play with the dog, and eat a Pop Tart. It comes down to our priorities.

This week, when the phone rings at an inconvenient time, and a voice says, "Hi, I'd like to talk to you about buying land in Nevada," use that moment (after you hang up) to say a prayer for someone in need. Use these robocalls as a reminder of the power of incessant, relentless, unceasing prayer; prayer that can not only soften the hardest of hearts, but can also bring strength in the face of great pain; prayer that never gives up . . . just like a telemarketer.

Changing the World
with a Five-Dollar Bill

"Never believe that a few caring people can't change the world. For, indeed, that's all who ever have."

—Margaret Mead

One December, we gave everyone in our church a $5 bill. It was not for brunch or a movie or a Powerball ticket (although the Powerball option was tempting). The money was for one purpose: to lift someone up. In short, everyone had to pay it forward. And so those $5 bills went out into the world and lifted up people from every walk of life . . .

One member took the $5 to 7-Eleven, bought five chicken wings, and gave them to a man who was curled up on the sidewalk outside with a sign that said, "I'm hungry."

Another went to Dollar Tree and used the money to buy mittens for a family in need.

Someone gave the $5 to a street vendor outside their apartment to help offset the cost of the fruit that had been stolen from his cart.

One woman used her $5 to help a struggling artist performing at the train station.

Yet another used hers to buy an umbrella for a homeless person on a rainy day.

One member used it to fund supplies for a woman in Afghanistan so that she might learn tailoring skills and eventually start a business.

And one person gave it to a waitress at lunch and said, "Take $5 off your next bill, then tell the customer why, and invite them to pay it forward in their own life."

This experience offered a powerful lesson on how to do a lot with a little. We don't need tons of money, a huge foundation, or an army of people to change the world. We can help others with tiny, personal gestures that show we care. Something as simple as helping someone feel heard or acknowledged can heal that person and enable him or her to go out into the world changed, ready to continue the chain of kindness.

It's like the dandelions many of us used to play with when we were little. You'd pick one up, make a wish, then blow the round fluffy ball of seeds at the top and watch as the wind transported them to reseed, replant, grow, and start again. That's exactly what we're talking about—the power of warmth, love, and compassion to reach out, to transform, to bring life.

But there's another lesson here too: to lift someone up, you have to be able to *find* someone to lift up. You have to get outside your own daily concerns to recognize the needs that surround us every day. Think of the examples above. You can't give money to help the fruit vendor if you aren't aware that he has experienced loss; you can't give food or an umbrella to homeless people if you don't notice them. To be able to give, you must first see the need.

When I was growing up, my parents always said to leave this world better than you found it. At the time, I thought they meant my room. But it's true in life as well. With one kind gesture at a time, we can leave this earth better than we found it.

Try it! Take a $5 bill and see what you can do to lift someone up. Hopefully, they will be inspired to do the same. With one kindness at a time, we can change the world. That's not some glib Hallmark statement. It's truth. We can, and together, we will.

There Are Angels in Manhattan

"Don't forget to show hospitality to the stranger, for you
may be entertaining an angel unawares."

—Hebrews 13:2

There are angels in Manhattan. Did you know that? Oh sure, they're
also in New Jersey and Georgia and Germany and Jaipur. But they
are in Manhattan . . . although no one believes it.

I find this hilarious since New York City is a place where you
can see anything and everything: a giant seventy-five-foot spruce
tree with twinkling Christmas lights in the middle of crowded,
bustling Rockefeller Center, a naked cowboy playing his guitar in
Times Square, a man walking down Wall Street in an expensive
three-piece suit and bunny ears, even Spider-Man playing the
saxophone in the Union Square subway station.

But angels? No.

It's understandable. Angels are a sneaky bunch. They like to
work incognito—under the radar. They operate in unexpected
places, through unassuming, everyday people like you and me, like
in the movie *Ghost*, where Whoopi Goldberg channels Patrick
Swayze. Any time there is an opportunity for a kind gesture,
miniscule as it may seem, angels will swoop in and make it happen.

Why? Because that's how you change the world. And this is not some Hallmark sentiment. This is scientific fact. An often-quoted theory known as the butterfly effect holds that a single occurrence, no matter how small, can change the course of the universe forever. For example, the flutter of a butterfly's wings in China can ultimately cause a hurricane in the Gulf of Mexico.

Of course, if the flutter of a butterfly's wings can change the course of the universe, how much more can the flutter of an angel's wings change? Tiny acts of kindness can reverberate throughout a person's life, throughout those around them, and, ultimately, throughout the world.

Think about the people in your life who have shown you a little kindness along the way. Then think about the effect that kindness had. Oprah Winfrey, for example, tells a story about her fourth-grade teacher, Mrs. Duncan. The young Oprah was scared to raise her hand in class, and it was Mrs. Duncan who helped her find the courage to answer, to be smart, to read, and to nurture her mind. We all know the rest of the story. A tiny act of kindness in an elementary school room in Nashville, Tennessee, truly changed the world.

It doesn't have to be Oprah. Recently, I was standing in line at a coffee vendor on 181st Street. An elderly woman in front of me ordered a coffee (price $1.50) and then slowly held up a quarter in payment. The vendor looked at her for a minute, and then, with an almost imperceptible smile, took the quarter and handed her the coffee. While the act itself may seem tiny, perhaps that coffee was the only "meal" she was to get that day.

We may never know the consequences of our actions, and we may never see the angels that swooped in and channeled their power through us in that moment, but they were there, and, in that moment, the angels made us part of something bigger and more powerful than anything we can imagine.

So I return to my original premise: there are angels in Manhattan. And Mississippi and Missouri and Montana. Believe it or not. It's up to you. But they are there, waiting and watching for an opportunity to change the world. The question is—will you play a part?

What Are You Getting the Baby Jesus for Christmas?

"There is a lot of bad 'isms' floating around this world, and one of the worst is commercialism."

—**Alfred, Macy's Janitor,** *Miracle on 34th Street*

Stampedes. Fist fights. Pushing and shoving.

Is it a political coup? A protest march? A Bette Midler concert?

No, it's Christmas shopping.

One would think that after two million years of evolution, human beings would have transcended such nonsense. Sadly, our lengthy holiday shopping lists continue to drive our fight-or-flight genes into a stress-fueled frenzy.

Everyone is included on these ridiculously long lists, from the paperboy to our co-workers to our great Aunt Else whom we haven't seen in years. Everyone, that is, except the most obvious person.

Here's a hint: look at the first six letters of the word: "CHRISTmas."

I am afraid that the baby Jesus gets the short end of the stick every year during the holidays. Given that we're celebrating his birthday, he should be the first person on the list!

What is the ultimate present to give the baby Jesus? And notice I said give him, not buy him. The best gifts are ones that have nothing to do with what money can buy.

The best gift guide I have found to date is contained in the book of Micah: "What does the Lord require of you but to do justice, love kindness and walk humbly with your God?" (Micah 6:8). So, how about putting acts of justice, kindness, and humility on your list? These are things that the baby Jesus would love way more than an Xbox.

Let's start with the gift of kindness. This one may be harder than we think. A *Consumer Reports* poll ranked "having to be nice" as one of our top ten holiday stressors. Seriously? We're not talking about winning the Nobel Peace Prize here, only a few modest acts of kindness.

Running short on "kindness" gift ideas? Consider the story of the Santa who learned sign language. Students from a local school for the deaf were invited to visit him, but they were not told that Santa knew sign language. When the first child climbed on his lap and saw him sign "What would you like for Christmas?" the child's face lit up.

While learning sign language would be at the top of a kindness gift list, you could also learn to speak to those who take the brunt of the holiday stress. For bus drivers, store clerks, waiters/waitresses, and others working similar jobs, being asked a simple question such as "How has your day been?" or "How are you doing?" shows that someone has noticed and cares. It doesn't take a lot. Find a way to reach out to people and give the gift of kindness.

In addition to kindness, we should consider giving the baby Jesus the gift of humility. The Chinese philosopher Lao Tzu explained the power of humility like this: "The rivers and seas lead the hundred streams, because they are skillful at staying low." This is such a beautiful image—streams flowing willingly into the rivers and seas, not because the rivers and seas hold themselves up, but because they lower themselves in the land, so that the water can naturally flow to them. We, too, might consider lowering ourselves so that we can better connect with others.

Looking for "humility" gift ideas? Try listening more. Everyone is dealing with something, although we may not see it immediately. People love to pretend that everything is perfect and lovely—God forbid we show vulnerability, or admit we need help. But notwithstanding the faces people show, everyone is fighting some type of battle, especially during the holidays, and the only way we'll see it is if we listen.

The author Anne Lamott suggests the acronym "W-A-I-T" as a listening tool. It stands for the question, "Why am I talking?" Pausing to listen to others is a great gift of kindness.

Finally, we should include the gift of "doing justice." Keep in mind that the scripture says, "Do justice." This is not a John Lennon song approach; it's not imagine justice. This requires action.

What are some "justice" gift ideas? Volunteer. One hour out of your week won't tick up your stress level that much. In fact, focusing on others might well reduce it. You could offer to spend your time wrapping gifts for children in shelters or writing holiday letters to our troops, veterans, and/or first responders. Maybe you could escort an elderly person to do some Christmas shopping or serve a hot meal on a cold day at a soup kitchen. Whatever it is, remember that a true holiday gift is an act of justice from one human being to another.

The bottom line? Put the baby Jesus on your Christmas list. His gift will be the easiest one to find, as it is simply about giving the gift of yourself. You don't have to risk the stampedes, fist fights, pushing, and shoving. Cultivate your sense of kindness, humility, and justice. Reach deep within and find what you have to give. As 1 Timothy 4:14 says, "Neglect not the gift that is within thee."

The Struggle Behind the Gift

"Being unwanted, unloved, uncared for, forgotten by everybody, I think that is a much greater hunger, a much greater poverty than the person who has nothing to eat."

—Mother Teresa

It's the time of year when traffic snarls, check-out lines explode to epic proportions, and shoppers channel characters from *Apocalypse Now*.

Ah, the angst of holiday shopping and the struggle behind the gifts.

But how about if we shift gears for a moment and move past the traffic, the lines, and the crazy shoppers to consider the true struggle behind the gifts?

Think about it like this. Have you ever sent a basket of fruit and nuts as a gift? It takes us about five minutes to order, but who performs the back-breaking work of harvesting the nuts? Who does the grueling dawn-to-dusk task of picking the fruit? If we look closely, we see that those who truly struggle are the Mexican and Central American farm workers who perform these demanding tasks, many under abusive conditions.

Let's try another scenario. What if we send a fancy box with gourmet chocolate and coffee? Who bears the struggle behind a gift like this? Who harvests your cocoa beans? Who does the physically exhausting work of drying and roasting the coffee beans? That struggle is borne primarily by millions of West African children forced into labor, some into slave labor.

These struggles aren't related only to fruits, nuts, coffee, and chocolate. Slave labor and abusive working conditions exist in the production of a wide array of holiday gifts, including toys, technology, textiles, and fashion.

Since about ten zillion Bible verses command us to help the oppressed, why not consider these four steps to satisfy our holiday giving and at the same time assist our brothers and sisters who bear the struggle? They're easy to remember because the first letters of the steps spell C-A-R-E.

C: CHOOSE YOUR GIFTS CAREFULLY

There are merchants who exploit workers and children for their cheap labor, and there are merchants who don't. In this age of the Internet, it takes about three minutes to check a company's record. For example, it took me about two and a half minutes to discover that LEGO recently signed a deal with UNICEF to promote children's rights and eliminate child labor. This information is easy to find. So choose your gifts carefully.

A: ACT

Why not donate to organizations that fight child slave labor or support migrant workers' rights? For example, if you are considering a gift for a child, you could buy a LEGO present, then make a side contribution to UNICEF. If the child receiving the gift is old enough, include a note explaining why you did it. That way, your gift is a learning experience for the child receiving it and an outreach to lift up struggling children.

R: REPORT

Take time out of your busy life to do a quick Google search about the reality of those who struggle behind your gifts. Educate yourself, then talk with your friends or share the information in your workplace. Reporting what we know about the plight of the oppressed is one of the most powerful ways to defend them.

E: EXERCISE YOUR RIGHT TO VOTE

The ex-governor of Minnesota, Jesse Ventura, once suggested that we make all politicians wear NASCAR suits. If you've ever seen a NASCAR suit, you know that the sponsors are clearly displayed, with the largest donors in the most prominent spots. Ventura suggested a NASCAR suit for politicians because, as he explained, "then we'll know who owns them."

When you vote, make sure that you know who owns your candidate. Is their largest contributor a company that is accused of using child labor or one that fights to alleviate it? When our voices come together on issues like this, we can truly effect change.

This season give your gifts, and give generously, but when you give, make sure that you C-A-R-E. Choose your gifts carefully, act to make a difference, report the issues, and exercise your right to vote.

Remember those who bear the true struggle behind the gift. For as the greatest giver of all taught us, "What you do for the least of them, you do for me" (Matthew 25:40).

Sun Mo Manger

"I never thought it was such a bad little tree. It's not bad at all, really. Maybe it just needs a little love."

—Linus Van Pelt, *A Charlie Brown Christmas*

"There's no room here or at the Holiday Inn, the Days Inn, or the C'mon Inn," the desk clerk said, shaking his head. "The Shriners have a gathering downtown, the Mary Kay convention is at the Coliseum, and there's a quilt show at the Marriott."

This was not welcome news. It was a cold autumn night in Bismarck, North Dakota. My husband Toby and I had finished a four-hundred-mile motorcycle ride from Wisconsin.

"Please . . . really . . . we'll take anything," I said, starting to worry.

"There is NO room here," he replied with an impatient tone. "The best you can do is ride up to Fort Mandan and try the Sunset Motel."

"But that's thirty miles!" I sighed.

"Yup," he said, "and you'd best hurry. They're gonna fill up, too."

Cold and exhausted, we fired up our Harley Road King and headed up the interstate to Mandan. As we crested the last hill before our exit, we saw the motel's flashing sign in the distance. It was an antiquated neon marker with some of the letters missing, so it read, "Sun Mo."

The woman behind the counter, gray hair to her waist, barked, "Can I help ya?"

"Y'all have any rooms?" I asked, praying fervently. "Last one," she said with pride, producing an old-timey key attached to a plastic teardrop-shaped medallion.

When we opened the door to the room, I immediately flashed to Luke's Christmas story because this—this was definitely a manger. I'm pretty sure the last guests to stay in that motel room were livestock. It was a tiny space with worn carpet, a cigarette-burned bedspread, and a sign in the bathroom that read, "Please don't use towels to clean guns."

We didn't care. We were out of the cold and in a place we could lay our heads. That was comfort enough.

It's a bad feeling to be left out in the cold—to be told there is no room at the inn, to be excluded, left out, or pushed aside. We've all been there.

Maybe it was early in life when someone didn't pick us for their sports team or failed to invite us to sit at their table during school lunch. Or maybe it was later when we were pushed aside for a job we wanted. Perhaps, we were dismissed or turned away because of our race, nationality, or religion. Or perhaps it was even later in life, when we felt left out or ignored because of age or illness.

The refrain "no room at the inn" is all too commonplace. For millions of American children, for example, there is no room at the "inn" of healthcare. For hundreds of thousands of Americans, the only room available is a homeless shelter. For millions of people globally, there is no room at the "inn" of food and sustenance.

Like Mary, Joseph, and baby Jesus, many of us have been turned away, but their story didn't end there, and neither does ours. In fact, the ending is the opposite. Through the power of love and mercy, Jesus became the one with the keys to the inn—the one who flung open the doors for all to find shelter.

We are all the beneficiaries of Christ's transformation. While we may be rejected by the world, we will never be rejected by its maker. Through that same love and mercy, we will always be welcomed and beloved as children of the most high: "Come unto me, all ye who labour and are heavy laden, and I will give you rest" (Matthew 11:28).

When we accept that gift, something amazing happens. Not to mix baby Jesus and Dr. Seuss, but *How the Grinch Stole Christmas!* explains it best: "They say—that the Grinch's small heart grew three sizes that day. And then—the true meaning of Christmas came through, and the Grinch found the strength of ten Grinches, plus two!"

Through the love and acceptance we receive, we are able to transform into the ones with the keys to the inn, the ones who share that love with our brothers and sisters, flinging open the doors for all to find shelter and rest.

For all those who feel left out this holiday season, for all those who have been excluded or rejected, for all those whose hearts and spirits are broken, there is good news this Christmas. For unto you is born this day the transformative gift of unconditional love—a savior, Christ the Lord.

JOY

Whoa!

"Let me keep my distance, always, from those
who think they have the answers.
Let me keep company always with those who say 'Look!'
and laugh in astonishment,
and bow their heads."

—Mary Oliver

If you ever want to get into the Christmas spirit fast, go to the Rockefeller Center Christmas Spectacular. They have *The Nutcracker*, dancing Santas, reindeer, and, of course, the famous Rockette dancers. But the thing that generates the most fun, at least for me, is watching the kids.

The last time I went, I was sitting near a little boy who was about five years old and there with his Dad. With every new thing that happened in the show, the little boy's eyes got huge, and he exclaimed, "Whoa."

A reindeer walked across stage. WHOA!

A Christmas tree started talking. WHOA!

The baby Jesus appeared in a manger with a giant star overhead. WHOA!

I was already excited enough, but to see the show through his eyes took it to a whole new level.

But then, there was his dad. While his young son was basking in what he saw as an avalanche of miracles, his dad was texting on a smartphone, uttering an occasional "Um-hum" or "Yeah, I see it." He missed the entire show.

What a sad example of how we adults come at the world, especially during the holiday season. We haul a heavy load of holiday stress. We hand-wring over worries about money, gifts, and who's coming to dinner. We carry the baggage of fear, judgment, and doubt—all things that block our ability to see the miracles of the season that are all around us. We lose that ability to look at the world like a little kid looks at Santa.

Dr. Randy Pausch, a professor at Carnegie Mellon who, after being diagnosed with terminal pancreatic cancer, gave a last lecture that went viral on YouTube. He framed the question in terms of characters from Winnie the Pooh. You may recall two of the characters: Tigger, the playful, positive, fun-loving tiger, and Eeyore, the pessimistic, negative, sad little donkey. Dr. Pausch said, "You just have to decide if you're a Tigger or an Eeyore. . . . Never lose the childlike wonder. It's just too important. It's what drives us."

Life is full of possibility. It's full of wonder and miracles, but we, in our doubt and cynicism, miss it. We live in a world where we think we have all the answers. We can split an atom, send a spacecraft to Mars, clone a sheep—what miracles are left?

There is at least one miracle left, and it's coming soon. In a short time, we will celebrate the gift of a tiny baby wrapped up and lying in a manger, a baby who ushers in a new world full of hope, love, and possibility rather than one of fear, doubt, or judgment. A world that we should all look upon with awe, a world that should make us all exclaim WHOA!

When you get a chance, stop your busy life for a minute or two, and watch some little kids. Maybe it's on the commute home or on the bus, at work, or while shopping. Find some little kids and watch their excitement and delight over the tiniest of things.

Then think about that little boy in the Christmas show. Let us not be like his father, oblivious to the miracles all around. Instead, let us see anew the Kingdom of God as it was meant to be seen—as a miracle, all around us, every day.

Look Homeward

"Well, time passed slowly. Rudolph existed the best he could. The snow monster kept him on the run, but once in a while, he would stop and make a friend or two. But it wouldn't last long, and Rudolph would be on his own again. But during all that time, a strange and wonderful thing was happening. Rudolph was growing up. And growing up made Rudolph realize you can't run away from your troubles. And pretty soon he knew where he had to go: home."

—Sam the Snowman,
Rudolph the Red-Nosed Reindeer (1964 TV Movie)

I live in New York City among steel and concrete mountains shrouded in smoke. They crowd me, their towering penthouse peaks stealing my light and air. Cold and soulless, they don't beckon or welcome me. They simply hold me captive as I hibernate, dreaming of other mountains.

About seven hundred miles south, those other mountains lie in wait. They, too, are shrouded in smoke. In fact, the Cherokee named them "Shaconage," land of the blue smoke. Those mountains don't crowd me, though; they swell my spirit. They don't steal my light and air; they create it. Teeming with soul and wisdom, the Blue

Ridge Mountains of North Carolina call me—constantly—to return home.

Those mountains are the ancient ones. Approximately 480 million years old, their highest points, originally higher than the Rockies, are now worn down to the elevation of Denver on the flat Colorado plains.

I was raised in the cradle of those old ones—on a farm burrowed in a mountain hollow along the French Broad River Valley, near the stone angel statue that inspired Thomas Wolfe's first novel, *Look Homeward, Angel.*

Watching over me was a protective ring of bald mountains and forested peaks with names like Mt. Pisgah, Caesar's Head, Graveyard Hill, and Black Balsam Knob. They tended me as I grew from seedling to sapling. They stood in knowing silence when I, like Thomas Wolfe, left to make my fortune in faraway lands with false mountains. And now the true mountains wait, tending to six generations of my Scotch-Irish-German ancestors, who rest in their hillsides covered with Appalachian soil at the feet of ancient, lichen-covered headstones bearing names like Whitmire, Glazener, Siniard, and Galloway.

Once a year or so, usually around the holidays, I emerge from my northern city prison and head south to remember the place from whence I came, always reserving a seat on the right-hand side of the plane so I can see the blue-misted peaks appear about an hour after takeoff. Every time that I return, those peaks offer a different blessing.

Sometimes it is a hike under an azure-colored sky along the high ridgeline of the Blue Ridge Parkway near the beautiful Pisgah Inn, or a close miss while fly-fishing for a feisty brook trout in a rushing eddy of the Davidson River. But then there are times when I come, my life knotted in worry and stress, and the peaks offer me the blessing of perspective. I am reminded of why I do things the way I do. The very manner in which I speak, sing, or think is a product of this history. Like an old hemlock, I am stabilized and strengthened by my roots.

As I begin hiking the damp, mossy, rhododendron-shaded trails, life shifts. Problems seem to fade into the sprawling green valley below. Stress becomes relative when I think about what those mountains have seen in their lifetime, what they have lived through, what they have survived. The mountains remind me of the long view—that each day is only a tiny snapshot in the panorama of life. I always leave their embrace with an emotional wind at my back, urging me forward.

What place feels the most like home for you? What calm and perspective does it bring? How do you carry it with you? Maybe one day I'll return to the Blue Ridge to live out my days, but if not, I'll return in the end, sprinkled as dusty food for that brook trout I couldn't catch, or as fertilizer for some lucky mountain laurel. It is then that I, too, will become one of the old ones, watching over my own.

What Am I Doing?

The holidays can add stress and confusion to life, but not enough to explain this unsettling thing I recently experienced . . .

I got up from my comfy seat by the Christmas tree, walked into the kitchen, and had no idea why I was there.

Have you had this happen? Please tell me yes.

For instance, yesterday as I walked into the kitchen, I stopped in the doorway and thought, "*What* am I doing?"

Was I hungry? No.

Did the plants need watering? No.

Was I there because I intended to clean? Definitely not.

I honestly couldn't remember. Then I began to think through what I had been doing up to that point. I was working on the computer in the living room, spilled some cranberry juice on my keyboard as I took a sip, and . . . paper towels! I needed paper towels.

Sometimes we have to look back in order to remember what we came to do.

The process of navigating our way through a forgetful mind is a metaphor for life. We sometimes lose our way, get confused about life and why we are here, and find ourselves saying, "What am I doing?"

It happens to everyone. And just like when you walk into a room and forget why you're there, the best way to remember is to ask yourself what you've been doing that has led you to this place. Take an inventory of your life, your choices, and your relationships. Look for the why. It works for everything from paper towels to existential questions of life.

For example, suppose you have a difficult job that you hate. If you're not sure why you're doing that job, consider that happiness is not necessarily driven by what we do. It's driven by the *why* behind it.

At the end of the day, ask yourself these questions: What good comes from this? Am I producing something that makes people's lives better or easier? Am I bringing home a check that pays for food and shelter for my family? Am I offering a co-worker friendship or healing? Find what matters in what you do. Then bring photos to work to remind you of those things. Keep them front and center.

Studies show that having a sense of purpose in life can improve your sleep quality and lower your risk of heart disease, stroke, and depression. It can build your self-esteem and self-confidence. Most of all, it brings direction, resilience, perspective, and joy. Without that knowledge, all we do is aimlessly put one foot in front of the other. As Mark Twain said, "The two most important days in your life are the day you are born and the day you find out why."

This exercise is not a one-shot deal, though; it's a lifelong task. Our sense of purpose changes as we progress through life. It can also get beaten up or stolen by outside voices. The world has a knack of pressing in, drowning out our sense of self and purpose with others' expectations about what is appropriate or right. That's why we must remind ourselves—every day—that our lives count for something and that we have a reason to get out of bed. As Jeremiah 1:5 reminds us, "Before I formed you in the womb, I knew you, and before you were born, I consecrated you."

Spend some time taking an inventory of your past. Think about where you've been, so you can remember what you came to do. And just in case you, too, walk into a room and forget why you came, ask yourself this: "What have I been doing that has led me to this place?"

It Is Enough

"This has too much cheese on it," said no one. Ever.

I love to cook. However, when I get in a kitchen, my family starts to worry. I am one of those people who think more is better.

For example, my signature dish is a cheese grit soufflé, and while the recipe is quite specific, I have trouble sticking with it. I always feel there needs to be more: *more* Velveeta, then *more* cheddar, then *more* garlic, then *more* salt, then *more* Velveeta, until I am left with a large pot of bubbling cheese goo.

If I were cooking for a starving mouse in a North Dakota blizzard, maybe it would make sense. Otherwise, I've ruined a delectable work of art.

The lesson? More is not better. If only I could remember that lesson in life! Perhaps this rings true with you as well? Do you ever think:

"If I had *more* money in the bank, things would be better."

"If I could get one *more* promotion at work, life would be better."

"If I could have *more* vacation time, *more* channels on my cable service, one *more* pair of Air Jordans under the Christmas tree, then my entire existence would be better."

We spend our lives chasing more. Yet, the things we chase will never complete us. Like that cheese grit casserole, more in life is not necessarily better. We don't have to add to the recipe for it to work. The recipe of life is enough. We are enough.

I am reminded of the story of Jesus' baptism. When he comes up out of the water, the spirit descends in the form of a dove, and a voice from heaven says, "This is my beloved, in whom I am well pleased" (Matthew 3:17).

We all yearn for those words. It feels great when we hear them, but when we don't hear them, our spirit withers. It's then that we must remember that if someone in your life doesn't call you beloved, it's their failing, not yours.

But hey, don't take it from me—believe the scriptures. Look again at Jesus' baptism. God didn't offer those healing words *after* Jesus had completed his ministry and was hailed as the Messiah. God offered Jesus those words *before* he began any of his work— before he called one disciple, preached one sermon, worked any miracles, or slapped down any demons. It was like God was saying, "It is enough. Your life is enough. You are enough."

It's the same for each of us. God whispers those affirming words to us long before our resume gets written. We are beloved not because of what we do, but because of who we are as children of God.

Tragically, those holy whispers tend to get shouted down by the evils of the world. We are surrounded by voices that tell us we're not enough, that we're lesser than. And, for many, those negative voices are amped up to a deafening decibel level.

Think about our brothers and sisters who are called lesser than based on race, sexuality, gender, or nationality. Or those who are deemed undeserving based on labels such as "immigrant." Or those who endure hatred and violence because they worship differently.

We must stop this horrible cycle of violence, and the only way we can do it is by pausing and remembering who we are. When we know we are beloved, when our hearts are full, there is no room for hatred, suspicion, or bigotry. Only then can we see that whether we are black, white, brown, Methodist, or Muslim, we are all beloved children in whom God is well pleased.

Before you begin your day, before you tackle anything on your to-do list, take a moment and listen. If you pay attention in those early hours, God's whisper—God's affirmation of your worth—will surely ring clear: It is enough. You are enough. You are my beloved in whom I am well pleased.

Never Postpone Joy!

"Every time a bell rings, an angel gets his wings."

—**Zuzu Bailey,** *It's a Wonderful Life*

To paraphrase Erma Bombeck, think of all the women on the Titanic who, on that fateful night, said no to dessert.

Okay, so we may not be on the Titanic, but sometimes life can make us feel like we are sinking, whether it's under the weight of holiday stress, work demands, family issues, medical problems, or difficult people. In those times of crisis, it's easy to forget dessert. To put it another way, it's easy to postpone joy.

We often think, "I'll get to it. I'll do it later. I'll be happy when X, Y, or Z happens," but as we defer happiness, time keeps ticking. Suddenly, we realize that years we can never get back have passed by while we were waiting for the right time. None of us have the luxury of putting off *anything*, especially joy! As the book of Proverbs tells us, "Do not boast about tomorrow, for you do not know what a day may bring" (Proverbs 27:1).

Let's take a moment to consider three strategies that can help us embrace rather than postpone joy. Since memory is not my forte, I'll frame them as an acronym: N-O-W.

N—Never ignore an opportunity to laugh! It's the most important healing tool we have. Sadly, thanks to low self-esteem or high self-doubt, some of us don't believe we deserve to be happy. So we bury our smiles and delay our joy. Newsflash: We deserve joy! We deserve to be happy. As Jesus taught, "I have told you these things so that you will be filled with my joy. Yes, your joy will overflow!" (John 15:11).

We deserve happiness. And not only do we deserve it, but when we claim our joy, we help others claim theirs too. As Louis Armstrong sang:

> "When you smilin', when you smilin'
> The whole world smiles with you.
> Yes, when you laughin', oh when you laughin'
> The sun comes shinin' through."

O—Observe. Many times, we opt for anger or resentment instead of joy, but if we take a moment to observe our situation closely, we may choose differently. The next time someone says something that makes you mad, ask yourself whether it was out of malice or ignorance. If it was malice, then walk away and protect your joy. If it was simple ignorance, then laugh at the mistake, correct the person if necessary, and go on your way. Either way, you will have chosen joy.

W—Wallow in gratitude. No matter where we find ourselves in life, there are things for which we should be grateful, even if it's simply opening our eyes in the morning. One of the best ways to remember our blessings is to start our day with a prayer of gratitude. The actor Denzel Washington once suggested a great way to ensure that prayer happens. He explained that you should put your shoes way under the bed at night because then, you've got to get down on your knees each morning to find them.

It's never too late to make a change. Years ago, a woman in our congregation adopted a dog from the local shelter. It was a cute collie/retriever mix that was within days of being euthanized. After the paperwork was done, she took him home and immediately named him "Just-in," for just-in-time.

Just-in's story is our story, too.

Maybe you feel stuck in a dead-end job. Maybe you've let your relationship fizzle out. Maybe you feel your dreams have faded or your sense of joy has disappeared.

Many of us are walking this earth physically alive but dead of spirit, operating at the level of our social security number—existing rather than living. But time is ticking. As my dear friend Rabbi Bob Alper warns, "When we are called to our maker, we will each be held responsible for all the opportunities for joy that we ignored."

The time to be happy is now.

The time to make positive changes for a better life is now.

Grab life's desserts! Laugh! And wallow in your opportunities for joy . . . while the opportunity is still here.

Healing the Humbug

"One moment can change a day,
one day can change a life,
and one life can change the world."

—Buddha

To add a little punch to this last meditation, grab a keychain or anything else that will make a rattling noise. Drop it on a hard surface for a sound effect every time you encounter the word "CHAINS."

One of my favorite Christmas movies is *Scrooge*. Not the newer versions. I love the one with the great British actor Albert Finney as Scrooge and Alec Guinness (Ben Kenobi in *The Empire Strikes Back*) as Marley, Scrooge's late business partner. As you probably remember, the movie is based on *A Christmas Carol* by Charles Dickens.

The story begins with Marley's ghost returning to warn Scrooge about the dangers of ignoring Christmas, forgetting charity and joy, and wrapping ourselves up in want and worry.

His ghost stands in Scrooge's bedroom, rattling his chains and wailing, "I wear the chain I forged in life. I made it link by link. Yard by yard. I girded it of my own free will, and by my own free will I wore it."

(CHAINS)

I know how he feels. Maybe you do, too. Have you ever gotten out of bed and felt like you were dragging three hundred yards of heavy iron chains with you? Maybe you were dragging the chains of self-doubt. Perhaps you were straining and pulling the chains of worry. You might have slogged through some days with the chains of greed and selfishness. Other days, you might have clanked around with the particularly heavy chains of anger, resentment, and fear. Scrooge knew all about that.

(CHAINS)

After Marley visits Scrooge, three additional ghosts (past, present, and future) appear to take Scrooge on a painfully raw inventory of his life, his choices, and his changes—all in an effort to warn him off his destructive path before it is too late.

The first ghost, the Ghost of Christmas Past, shows Scrooge how he began to forget Christmas early on in his life. He chose work and money over love, family, and happiness. "Humbug!" he would say to these things. "Bah, humbug."

The second ghost shows him that as the years went by, those choices changed him. Scrooge watches how he became withdrawn, sullen, selfish, and judgmental. Over time, he turned into a person who resented the happiness of those around him. He became a person who couldn't feel joy.

Then the scariest of all—the Ghost of Christmas Yet to Come— arrives to show him that those changes will have consequences. For example, in this future world, Tiny Tim dies because Scrooge doesn't pay his dad enough to get medical care. But the suffering isn't only about others. The last thing the ghost shows him is a graveyard, where a cheap tombstone on an isolated, unkept grave bears his name.

We see Scrooge's life as a chain reaction of choices, changes, and consequences, and in the end, Scrooge's chain is far longer than Marley's.

(CHAINS and add a "Humbug!")

I'd like to say that we can leave that scary moment at the movie theater, but in fact, we forge the same chains in life. We all make choices, some good and some bad, and that's fine. But when we continually repeat the bad choices, that's when we forge the first link. And over time, that link becomes two links, then three, then ten, then fifty. And before you know it, you're dragging one heavy weight.

It's then that your mood and personality start to change. People around you begin to be affected. And to all things good and true, you say "Humbug!" As the great essayist and philosopher Ralph Waldo Emerson said, "[I]t behooves us to be careful what we worship, for what we are worshipping, we are becoming."

Dickens was right—for Scrooge and for all of us. Every once in a while, we must take a "Marley test." We must periodically ask ourselves this: If we were visited by the ghost of our Christmas past, the ghost of *our* Christmas present, and the ghost of *our* Christmas future . . . what would we see? What choices have we made over the years? What have we prioritized? And, most importantly, if we keep going down the same path, where will we end up?

(CHAINS)

These are sobering questions, but here's the good news. The story doesn't end at the cheap tombstone on an isolated, unkept grave. There is still a chance to heal the humbug.

Ultimately, Scrooge awakes with his arms wrapped around his bedpost and realizes that he has gotten his wish. He has gotten a second chance! And from that moment on, he lives differently, sees the world differently, treats other and himself differently.

The moral of the story? It's never—ever—too late to change. I don't care how old you are, how entrenched you've become, or how many chains you have forged. It's never too late to alter a decision, change your mind, make amends, take a new path, pursue a long-lost dream, or find love again. Re-evaluating our choices and priorities is like adjusting the rudder of a great ship. The slightest movement can change its entire course.

Sometime today, set aside a few moments to take the Marley test. Look at your past choices, your present priorities, and the future consequences of both.

(*CHAINS*)

If you don't like what you're seeing, then remember it's not the end of the story.

We can find hope again. We can change our ways. We can change our life and thus change our world. All we have to do is tap into that place in our hearts that is full of good tidings and great joy.

All we have to do is heal the humbug.

CHRISTMAS DAY

All God Wants for Christmas is You!

"I just want you for my own
More than you could ever know.
Make my wish come true
All I want for Christmas is you."

—Mariah Carey

Here we are on Christmas day—which means that by now, we've all heard Mariah Carey's song approximately 57,000,000 times.

Every day.

Everywhere.

At CVS and Walmart. At Ace Hardware and Macy's. Even the Salvation Army volunteers play it on the corner as they collect money.

To which song am I referring?

"All I Want for Christmas is You."

If this doesn't sound familiar, then apparently, you have not left your home in the past twenty-five years. This catchy holiday love song from 1994, which reminds us about the joy of reuniting with loved ones, has sold over sixteen million copies.

But here's a twist. What if we took this ubiquitous song and made it an anchor—a reminder of something deeper than human love? What if we heard it as a love song from God?

Sounds kind of crazy, right? God singing Mariah Carey's song to us? But the lyrics are spot on, as God longs to reunite with us. As Ezekiel 34:11 explains, "For thus says the Lord God: I myself will search for my sheep, and will seek them out."

It's true. God yearns to be with us—at all times, in all places.

Consider what happened a few years ago at the Holy Child Jesus Church in Richmond Hill, Queens. Jose Moran, the custodian, had finished setting up the Nativity scene and gone to lunch. When he returned about an hour later, he heard the cry of an infant. He went into the sanctuary and found a tiny baby boy, umbilical cord still attached, swaddled in purple towels on the floor of the manger.

Later, the police identified camera footage from a local 99-cents store that showed a young mother with a baby; she was buying purple towels. Minutes after being filmed at the store, she appeared at the church and laid the baby, swaddled in the purple towels, in the church Nativity scene. The congregation named the baby "Emmanuel," Hebrew for "God with us."

Here is the Christmas story retold in the twenty-first century: a young mother (perhaps single and unwed) gives birth in dire circumstances, wraps a baby boy in swaddling clothes, and lays him—literally—in a manger. What's even more poignant is that the baby is wrapped in purple towels (the color of royalty) that were purchased from a 99-cents store.

Like the Christ child, that little boy entered the world wrapped in shame, abandonment, fear, and loneliness. That's how God chooses to enter the world—in our deeply broken places, in the places where we think there is no hope, in the crevices and corners where there seems so possibility of joy. And because we are offered healing in those places, we must, in turn, shine God's light into the broken places of the world.

Recently, I met someone who did exactly that. It happened while I was in line at Walgreens. I was behind an elderly Russian woman who was bent over a walker packed with plastic bags that were stuffed to the brim. For several minutes, she shuffled through the bags looking for her wallet, and as the line got longer, people got more aggravated.

All of a sudden, a tall, smiling man with a Walgreens nametag reading "Ababacar" walked up to her. He turned out to be the manager of the store and was from Senegal. When she saw him, a huge smile broke across her face. He called her by name, gave her a hug, helped her find her wallet, and walked her to the door.

I found out later that she lived by herself above the store, and that he'd been helping her for years, including preparing food and bringing her medicine. When I thanked him for what he'd done, he simply said, "If we don't care for each other . . . who are we?"

Of course, that's easier said than done. It's easy to turn away when the pain or suffering we see is alien to us or in a faraway land, but that's no excuse. Just as God has healed us, we must share that healing with others.

Try this: When you read the paper or watch the news, take note of how you react to stories of pain in our world. If you shrug off someone else's pain, ignore it, or don't feel much emotion, then change the demographics of the story. Make the person in the story resemble you—your race, your ethnicity, your nationality, your religion. How would you feel then? What if you changed the location? What if this happened in your home, to your family? Does that alter your perspective?

It is in the broken places where the Christ child truly dwells. Let us look for him there. Let us search for him in the fragmented places of our lives. Let us seek him in the shattered places in our world—in the hospitals and prisons, in the shelters and soup kitchens, in the bullets and bombs. If we truly seek Emmanuel, we should look for him not in the glitz or glamor of our modern Christmas celebrations, but in an abandoned newborn lying in a plywood manger, wrapped in purple towels from a 99-cents store.

On this Christmas Day, remember you are a beloved child of God, and if you doubt that, then listen to Mariah Carey's song and imagine it as a love song to you from God.

Like the Christ child, God yearns to be with you. Whoever you are, wherever you are, God is longing for you. And when you feel that love—truly, deeply, and honestly—you will yearn to share it with others.

Commit to bringing joy to the world. Be a blessing for everyone you meet. Live each day knowing you are part of something greater.

Remember that you are loved. You are claimed. You are never alone.

Because all God wants for Christmas is you!

AFTER CHRISTMAS

Taking Down the Tree

There is one holiday ritual I hate: taking down the tree. It's a sad job, as it marks the end of the season. It's also messy. Dragging out a month-old, dried-up balsam means getting sticky needles everywhere. Most of all, it leaves the house with this big empty hole in the corner of the living room.

What was there before the tree? I can't even remember, but I took the tree down, and here I sit, feeling sad, staring at a bare spot in the living room and a house strewn with needles.

I need to get over this annual trauma. January is supposed to be the month of moving on, cleaning out, and lightening up, right? Perhaps if I thought of taking down the tree as a New Year's resolution exercise, it would be easier.

New Year's invites us to think of things like my tree—the old, dried-up parts of our lives that need clearing out. Maybe we need to release a grudge, a lingering sense of self-doubt, or even a dream that has died. Whatever it is, just like taking down the tree, letting go can bring a renewed sense of possibility and freedom.

For example, the hole in the corner of my living room can now accommodate a floor lamp to light the room or a plant to bring life and energy to the house. What things in your life are past their time? What things are taking up room without bringing light or life?

Of course, even if we know what needs to go, we may avoid clearing it out because letting go can leave a hole we're not sure how to fill. If we let go of anger, for example, what goes in its place? If we aren't mad, then who are we? If we forgive, does that mean the deed goes unpunished?

We may also avoid clearing out an old Christmas tree because it can be messy. When you leave the tree up too long, needles begin to fall everywhere. Worse, they end up in strange places you didn't expect—like the needles I found in the vegetable bin of the refrigerator last May. In the same way, when we let a painful or difficult issue sit too long, the "needles" or fallout from that issue can find their way into strange places, producing anger or tears at unexpected times. Best to deal with the issue now.

The new year is an opportune time to revisit our priorities and sense of purpose. What blessings do you want to invite into your life now that you've made room? How about forgiveness? By letting go, you're not condoning the act, only releasing the heavy burden of bitterness. As the old saying goes, the most influential person in your life is the one you refuse to forgive. Or how about welcoming peace into your life? If you let go of worry by trusting in a higher power, you can put your heart at rest.

Miraculous things can happen when we make room. As the book of Isaiah teaches, "Do not remember the former things, or consider the things of old. I am about to do a new thing; now it springs forth, do you not perceive it? I will make a way in the wilderness and rivers in the desert" (Isaiah 42:18-19).

Hard as it was, I guess I'm glad I took down the tree. Sure, I have a lot of needles to sweep and furniture to rearrange, but hey, if I didn't take down the old dried-up tree, then where would I find room for the new tree—and the new joy—next Christmas?

Happy New Year's cleaning to you all!

KEEP IN TOUCH!

I hope you have enjoyed my book and found some new gratitude and joy in your life. Now we've got to keep it going! Here are some ways:

SIGN UP for my FREE bi-weekly newsletter, the *Shiny Side Up*, which shares infectious inspiration that will lift you up, make you smile, and leave you stronger! http://susansparks.com/connect/

ENROLL in one of my new ECOURSES on the healing power of humor. http://susansparks.com/online-courses/

READ more of my books. Try my award-winning first book *Laugh Your Way to Grace: Reclaiming the Spiritual Power of Humor*. Featured by *O, The Oprah Magazine*, this book shares a humorous, yet substantive look at the power of humor in transforming our life, work, and spiritual path.

Or my second book featured by *The Christian Citizen: Preaching Punchlines: The Ten Commandments of Comedy*, which shares how the tools of standup comedy can transform preaching – and all forms of communication.

WATCH and LISTEN to my weekly sermon broadcast LIVE every Sunday at 11a.m. EST from the historic Madison Avenue Baptist Church in New York City.
http://mabcnyc.org/worship/live-streaming/
Or subscribe to our sermon podcast and listen later at your convenience.

LIKE/FOLLOW my Facebook and Instagram pages (links on SusanSparks.com) where you'll find more joy and gratitude ideas. And maybe consider sharing about the book on social media! There is a sample chapter on my website you can share with your friends. Access it at http://susansparks.com/books/miracle-on-31st-street/

SHARE. If this book has brought joy to your life, share it with others. Show them some love! Send them a note, tell them how much they mean to you, and include the gift of Christmas cheer any time of the year (or at least let them borrow the book ☺).

POST A REVIEW. If you enjoyed the book (or even if you didn't) I would so appreciate you posting a review on Amazon! Honest reviews are super important for the success of the book. So take a moment and please add your opinion! MANY thanks!

GATHER. Form a reading group in your community and use the book, free Advent calendar, and workbook journal to spark some wonderful conversations.

INVITE me to guest preach or speak (live or virtual) in your community! I'd love to share some joy!

For more ways to keep in touch, check out my website: SusanSparks.com.

I look forward to hearing from you!

AND make sure you have downloaded the workbook and free advent calendar HERE: http://susansparks.com/books/miracle-on-31st-street/

AUTHOR BIO

As a trial lawyer turned standup comedian and Baptist minister, Susan Sparks is America's only female comedian with a pulpit. A North Carolina native, Susan received her B.A. at the University of North Carolina, law degree from Wake Forest University, and her Master of Divinity at Union Theological Seminary in New York City.

Currently the senior pastor of the historic Madison Avenue Baptist Church in New York City (and the first woman pastor in its 170-year history), Susan's work with humor, healing, and spirituality has been featured in *O, The Oprah Magazine;* the *New York Times;* and on such networks as ABC, CNN, CBS, and the History Channel.

A featured TEDx speaker and a professional comedian, Susan tours nationally with a stand-up Rabbi and a Muslim comic in the Laugh in Peace Tour. In addition to her speaking and preaching, Susan writes a nationally syndicated column through Gannett distributed to over six hundred newspapers reaching over twenty-one million people in thirty-six states.

In addition to *Miracle on 31st Street*, she is the author of two other books, *Laugh Your Way to Grace: Reclaiming the Spiritual Power of Humor* and *Preaching Punchlines: The Ten Commandments of Standup Comedy.*

Most importantly, Susan and her husband, Toby, love to fly-fish, ride their Harleys, eat good BBQ, and root for North Carolina Tarheel basketball and the Green Bay Packers.

Find out more about Susan at SusanSparks.com!

Made in the USA
Monee, IL
05 March 2021